THE NERD HERD

~~B~~CHook 2

For Carissa, a kindred spirit and an udderly terrific friend—NL

For Sooze, thanks for getting us through 2020 in one piece! Love—CK

Scholastic Australia
An imprint of Scholastic Australia Pty Limited
PO Box 579 Gosford NSW 2250
ABN 11 000 614 577
www.scholastic.com.au

Part of the Scholastic Group
Sydney • Auckland • New York • Toronto • London • Mexico City • New Delhi • Hong Kong • Buenos Aires • Puerto Rico

Published by Scholastic Australia in 2021.

Cover design by Hannah Janzen.
Internal design by Elly Whiley.

A catalogue record for this book is available from the National Library of Australia

ISBN: 978-1-76097-461-9

Typeset in Apertura, Blorp, Knicknack, Agent 'C' and Pequena Pro.
Printed in China by Hang Tai Printing Company Limited.
Scholastic Australia's policy, in association with Hang Tai Printing Company Limited, is to use papers that are renewable and made efficiently from wood grown in responsibly managed forests, so as to minimise its environmental footprint.

10 9 8 7 6 5 4 3 2 1 21 22 23 24 25 / 2

THE NERD HERD

RAGING WOOL

Book 2

NATHAN LUFF

CHRIS KENNETT

A Scholastic Australia book

THE NERD HERD

PREVIOUSLY . . .

We'd done the impossible: a lamb, a llama, and a goat had sent a fox scampering away from the petting zoo, her bushy tail between her legs. No longer would people think we were meek, helpless creatures.

We were **fierce**.
We were **ferocious**.
We were **The Woolly Bullies!**

Oh, I should probably mention the minor incident where we removed an electric fence from a bull's pen. I'm sure it's completely unrelated, but, somehow, the bull escaped.

I should probably *also* mention that the bull has severe **behavioural issues**, so it's not really great that he's now dangerously on the loose.

Oops.

CHAPTER ONE

TAKING STOCK

T-Bone mustn't have heard the news about how **fierce** and **ferocious** we are, or else he wouldn't have charged at us as we tried to enter the barn.

I did what any brave lamb would do. I sprang on his back and rode him like I was a cowboy at a rodeo. He bucked and tried to throw me but I held on tight.

I rode him all the way back to his pen, where I jumped free and clamped the gate shut.

Although, that might not be *exactly* true. OK, that didn't happen at all. Maybe it was more like this:

Shaama, Billy and I ran faster than we'd ever run before. We ducked behind our regular tree, panting like **thirsty dogs**, and waited a full minute before poking our heads back around.

We hadn't been followed.

'Well, this is a disaster,' I said. 'We only just showed everyone how impressive **The Woolly Bullies** are when we got rid of the fox.'

'I thought we were **The Nerd Herd**,' Billy said. 'That's what everyone's calling us. It's catchy.'

'Ugh! The point is, the barn should be ours!' I said.

The barn was warm and cozy, with a fire that burned all day and night.

Ringo, the farm dog, and **Plus-Sized Puss** were the ones who usually bullied us out of the barn, but now **T-Bone** had taken over.

It wasn't fair!

'Don't blame me,' Shaama said. 'It was your idea to move the electric current off T-Bone's fence.'

I sighed. 'We *all* forgot to put it back on. This certainly is a **regret-a-bull** situation.'

Shaama, who can't handle the fact that I'm a **pun master**, spat in my face.

'**Shaama Llama Ding Dong!**' I cried. I only use her full name when I'm angry.

'Yes, Baaaaaarnabus,' she said, preparing to spit again.

'You're perfectly aware there's only one *a* in Barny!' I huffed.

'Look at me!' Billy shouted, diverting our attention. 'Look at me!! **Look at me!!!**'

I know that Billy is a young goat, so he's technically a *kid*, but still, is that really an excuse to act like a *kid*?

'I look **ridiculous**,' Billy said. 'I did not get **egged** and **electrocuted** just so that we would be back in the exact same situation we were in before. I need a brush, and that bull needs to get out of my barn. In that order!'

Shaama hurried away to her **special tree**. She uses a hollowed-out section to store various things she finds—things she thinks might one day be useful.

Just between you and me, Shaama has a **hoarding problem**.

She returned quickly, placing something down behind Billy. I scrunched up my face.

'I think it's the ribcage of a **dead rat**,' Shaama whispered before raising her voice for Billy to hear. 'It's an **antique ivory hairbrush** that I picked up the other day.' Shaama winked at me.

Billy lay down. 'Antique? Ivory? I suppose it will do then. Proceed, but be gentle. I do bite.'

Billy had never let us brush him before. He claimed his **angora coat** of mohair was too delicate for anyone untrained to handle.

Shaama and I took turns trying to pull the dead rat's ribcage through Billy's tangled fleece. It was impossible to be gentle and, after a while, we gave up trying.

Instead, one of us held Billy down while the other combed. I've never been to a beauty salon, but I'm pretty sure that's how they do it anyway.

With a bit of effort, I managed to tune out Billy's screams.

Half an hour later, Billy was looking exactly like himself again.

Even his fringe looked normal after we accidentally pulled out all the stained hairs.

'Enough! Go deal with the bull,' Billy said.
'Umm, shouldn't we all be dealing with the bull?' I said.
'I'm too traumatised. I'll offer encouragement from the side, like a **cheerleader**. I'm very beautiful—I'd make a great cheerleader!'

Shaama shrugged. 'The humans will wake soon. They'll take T-Bone back to his pen.'

That didn't feel right. **The Woolly Bullies** wouldn't hide behind a tree and wait for the humans to fix it. That's something **The Nerd Herd** would do.

‘But what if there was a way we could get T-Bone back into his pen ourselves?’ A wild smile took over my face. ‘We’d be **legends**, wouldn’t we?’

‘Oh dear. What exactly are you thinking?’ Shaama asked.

CHAPTER TWO

SETTING THE TRAP

There was no point getting T-Bone back to his pen if he could easily escape again. First, we had to get the electric fence back up and working to contain him. It was still connected to the chicken coop, where we'd left it.

Shaama double and triple checked that everything was switched off before she tapped the wires with her hoof. Nothing happened and we all started breathing again.

'It made a strange sound last night before it stopped working,' I said as we gathered up the power box and wires. 'Are you sure you can fix it?'

The chooks had been watching us closely. Now, Rhonda, Alice and Lyn rushed over in a flap.

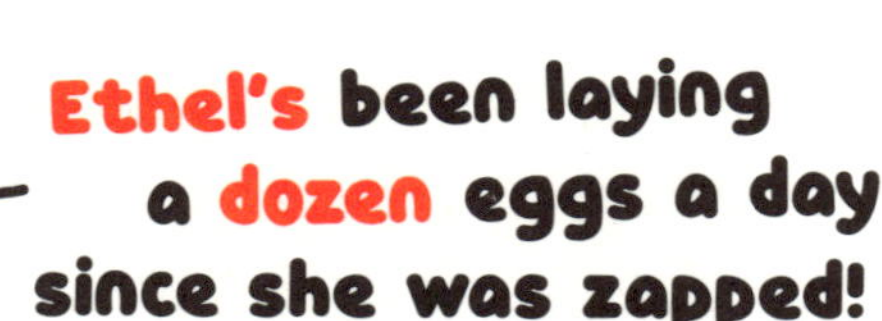

Personally, I think it's embarrassing how she's acting like a spring chicken all of a sudden.

It's not fair! We all want a go at being zapped!

'Sorry, ladies,' I said, backing away. 'We have more important business at hand.'

I turned to Shaama. 'So, can you fix it or not?'

'I'm sure I have some spare parts in my trunk that will get this back up and running,' Shaama said.

I know what you're thinking: *What is she doing collecting spare electrical parts? And how does she even know what to do with them? Isn't she a* ***llama?***

'You're very smart,' I said. 'You must also have a few **dip-llamas** stored in your trunk, huh?' Shaama hurried off and I had to run to catch up.

She stopped suddenly and I crashed into her back.

I scratched my head. I never knew Shaama hung out with other animals. I thought she was always with us. You learn new things every day!

When T-Bone had first escaped, he didn't go through the gate. He'd trampled one of the side fences and so our first job was to fix it. Shaama and I stood the fallen fence post back up and secured it into place with dirt and rocks.

Billy was no help. With his mohair brushed, his long-flowing fringe once again fell over his eyes. He sat at a distance, offering words of encouragement to what he thought was us. In actual fact, it was a very **confused pigeon**.

The electric motor and wires were easy to reattach. But the hard part was getting the whole system working again. Shaama fetched some parts from her trunk and tinkered with the power box for quite some time. Finally, she gave it a kick and the fence spluttered out its usual **electrical hum**.

I shuddered. I'd once felt that hum pass through my entire body.

Shaama nodded her satisfaction and turned it off. 'We'll turn it back on once he's inside,' she said.

Speaking of which, I noticed that with the fence now fixed and the gate still closed, there was no way of actually getting **T-Bone** back inside his pen.

A slight **flaw** in our plan.

Being able to install and repair electrical equipment is impressive but there is **nothing** more complicated for a farm animal than opening a gate. It's a hoof thing.

We needed something long and skinny to reach through and lift the latch off. Billy's **horns** were long and skinny.

He was still offering words of encouragement to the pigeon when we grabbed him.

'What's happening?' he yelled. 'Let me go! I'm not with them, I'm only the **cheerleader!**'

Owww, that hurts.
My horns are purely
decorative!

The latch came off, the gate swung open and our trap was set.

We dropped Billy.

He tried biting us but bit the poor pigeon instead.

'All we need to do now is get T-Bone in here, then, **BAM**, we close the gate and **ZAP**, we turn the electricity back on,' I said. Shaama nodded. 'Right, and how exactly do we get him down here?'

It was a very good question.

We came up with a lot of plans. Most were not good. One was less not-good than the others, so we named it our **Master Plan**.

THE NOT-GOOD PLANS:

* We attach chains to T-Bone and learn to drive the tractor
* We hypnotise T-Bone
* We dress up as a beautiful cow and make T-Bone follow us.

THE LESS NOT-GOOD PLAN: (AKA THE MASTER PLAN)

* We lay down a trail of bull-treats along the path and wait until T-Bone follows them back into his pen.

'Right, OK,' I said. 'We will make this work.'
'Wait, what exactly are bull-treats?' Billy asked.

That was another very good question . . .

CHAPTER THREE

TRAIL OF TREATS

‘What do bulls like?’ I asked the others.

We paced back and forth, thinking. Blinded by his fleece, Billy ran into the fence and decided to think sitting down instead.

'Don't bulls chase **red capes** and flags?' I said. 'They must like the colour **red**. We could lay out a trail of red things. Rose petals and . . .' I couldn't think of anything else red. Rose petals seemed a bit **romantic**. T-Bone didn't seem like the **romantic** type.

‘Well, he’s going to get hungry at some stage, isn’t he? So what do bulls eat?’ I asked.
‘Hay,’ Shaama said.

What followed was quite a frustrating conversation between Shaama and me:

Yes, hey what?

No, I said *hay!*

Yes, I'm listening, you have my attention . . . hey what?

HAY, THAT'S IT, YOU IDIOT!

No need to yell or use names, I can hear you. Hey what? What do you want to tell me?

BULLS EAT HAY!

We tore a hay bale apart with our teeth. By we, I mean Shaama and me. Billy watched. Well, no, he didn't. He sat, not-watching, while we did the hard work.

'Yay, you can do it,' he muttered with no enthusiasm.

Worst. Cheerleader. Ever.

We took the hay and scattered it in a path between the barn door and T-Bone's pen. When we'd finished, we collapsed next to Billy in exhaustion.

'That's it, keep going. You're doing a good job,' Billy said, yawning.

I guess I thought T-Bone would smell the hay and come investigate.

He didn't.

Shaama and I stood outside the barn and had a fake conversation in really loud voices.

Wow, look at all this delicious-looking hay just sitting here.

Yes. This is the most delicious hay I have ever seen.

Nothing from T-Bone.

'One of us needs to go in there,' I whispered. Shaama nodded and we both looked at Billy. 'Keep going. You're great,' he muttered.

We didn't need a **cheerleader**. What we needed was someone to **prod** T-Bone into action. And it was about time Billy did something useful.

We pretended that we'd given up and started walking away, guiding the half-blind Billy between us.

Only we hadn't given up. And we weren't walking away.

Shaama and I stopped either side of the barn door, and Billy, totally unaware of what was happening, walked right into our trap.

A few seconds later, Billy came rushing out, screaming, with T-Bone in pursuit. Shaama and I once again flanked him either side as we guided him along the bull treat path. Our plan was to hide as soon as T-Bone lowered his head to start eating.

But T-bone didn't stop to eat the hay.
He didn't even notice the hay.
He kept charging and he was **fast**.
Super fast.

One thing was clear—there was no way we'd make it to his pen in time.

'This was a **mis-steak**,' I shouted. You know, there really isn't a bad time for a good pun. Despite our predicament and speed, Shaama still managed to spit in my face.

'What is happening?' Billy screamed.

I spotted Ringo, watching from behind a fence. 'Ringo, help!' I shouted.
T-Bone came to a sudden halt, digging his rear feet into the road and sending a spray of rocks flying over us.

When the dust died down we could see T-Bone eyeing off Ringo.
GRUNT!

Ringo **yelped**.

T-Bone **charged**.

The fence in between Ringo and T-Bone was no match for the bull. It crumbled easily. Ringo was **fast** though, and **crafty**. He took a path through holes in other fences and soon he'd disappeared.

Snorting, T-Bone spun around in circles, trying unsuccessfully to find his enemy.

Eventually he gave up. He backtracked and **stomped** right over the broken fence. Shaama, Billy and I were standing ready to continue the chase but he gave us only a brief glance before lowering his head to eat the hay.

He followed the trail of hay all the way back to the barn.

CHAPTER FOUR

AN UNLIKELY ALLIANCE

Shaama laughed. 'We almost got trampled. T-Bone is still in the barn and I imagine Billy now has trust issues.'

'Wait, what? Why would I have—**did you lead me into the barn on purpose?**' Billy said, horrified.

'No, no, no, of course not.' I flared my eyes at Shaama. 'This is brilliant news because we learnt something valuable—'

'No. We learnt that T-Bone **hates** Ringo,' I said. 'Even more than he hates us.'

'Of course he does. Everyone hates Ringo,' Shaama said.

'So . . . that means we can use Ringo as **bait** to lure T-Bone out of the barn and get him where we want him.'

Shaama laughed again. 'Oh yeah, right, and how exactly do we get Ringo to go along with *our* plan?'

Ringo was half-in and half-out of his doghouse. That's right—he has his own house and yet he is still always hogging the barn. Typical.

Ringo didn't even acknowledge my presence.

'I was just in the neighbourhood and thought I'd pop in. Wow, I don't think I've ever been this close before. I like what you've done with all those **half-eaten bones**. Very shabby chic. And what is that . . . **unique smell?** Is it purely decaying meat or have you added a little something special?'

Ringo's top lip curled up. 'Oh, no, I like it. I'm thinking of getting a scented candle just like it actually . . .' I said.

'Right, well, I couldn't help but notice you've been having a **ruff day**.' I paused for Ringo to fully appreciate how funny I am. A **growl** started building in Ringo's throat. 'Aren't farm dogs supposed to chase the cattle and not the other way around?'

Ringo pounced on me and I was unprepared for the assault. He had my neck in his mouth and I could feel his teeth pressing in. His **putrid dog breath** made my eyes water.

Ringo released me, but very slowly. Strings of saliva connected us until eventually they snapped. Somehow I managed not to vomit.

'Well?' Ringo said.

'If we can get T-Bone back in his pen, us Woolly Bullies–'

'**The Nerd Herd** is what they're calling you,' Ringo interrupted.

I laughed. 'I don't think anyone's actually using that name, are they? Anyway, what I'm saying is that we can activate the electric fence and keep T-Bone contained there. The only problem is, getting him there . . .'

'How does this concern me?' Ringo asked, settling down for a nap.

'Don't you want to teach T-Bone a lesson? Show him who's boss?' I said.

'Just spit it out. What do I have to do?' Ringo growled, one eye open.

I limped back to Shaama and Billy. The leg that Ringo had bitten was throbbing.

'What is that stench?' Billy asked. Ringo had dragged me all over his disgusting doghouse and now my wool stank of dog.

It gave me an idea.
A **brilliant idea!**

'So, what did he say?' Shaama said.
'He declined the offer to be the bait, but it's OK because who needs the real Ringo? We only need T-Bone to **think** it's Ringo. I already smell like him and so now, I will **be** Ringo!'

Who would ever believe that you are a dog?

I gave a brilliant demonstration:

'See, it's easy,' I said.

CHAPTER FIVE

A SHEEP DOG

T-Bone isn't blind, so I needed a **Ringo-disguise**.

'Say no more,' Shaama said and led both Billy and me to her tree trunk of treasures.

She started pulling out random things: plastic bags, empty snack wrappers, broken toys, batteries, rope, a child's beanie.

'Why on earth do you collect these things?' I asked. 'When are you ever going to need a child's beanie? You're what they make beanies out of!'

'There is nothing wrong with being prepared for any situation,' Shaama said.
'Well, it looks like you're preparing for a **llama-ggedon**,' I said. I waited for my friends to start laughing uncontrollably at my joke and yet, for some unexplainable reason, they ignored me. 'You do get it, don't you?'

Shaama took the child's beanie and forced it on me, pulling it down so that it covered my entire head.

'Oh look, the beanie has proven useful after all,' she said.

Soon I was ready. Well, as ready as I was ever going to be.

Shaama had used charcoal to give me the same coloured markings as Ringo. She'd also made a collar from some chip packets and tied on a dog tail that she'd torn off a stuffed toy.

'Wow, you look just like him,' Shaama said.

I didn't. At all.

Thankfully, it would be dark in the barn. I sent Shaama down to the pen, ready to activate the electricity as soon as T-Bone was inside.

'Cheerleading?' I said. 'We don't need a **cheerleader**. We need someone who actually **helps**.'

'I help. Never underestimate the power of **encouragement**. You know, you are so brave, Barny. Sooooo brave. You can do this on your own. You let that bull know who runs this place, OK?' Billy cheered.

'See—encouragement is very helpful. I just convinced you to do something **stupid**,' Billy smiled.

‘What? Does that mean you don’t think I can do this?’

‘You’re a **tiny lamb**. He’s a **ferocious bull** . . . so . . . of course you can’t—I mean, yes, you can totally do this. **Go Barny!**’ Billy cheered.

Shaking only slightly, I backed myself through the barn door, wanting to be facing the exit at all times.

The fire had died down overnight but it still sent flickering shadows across the walls. There were mysterious brown discs—kind of like **enormous cookies**—scattered on the ground like landmines, obstructing my way.

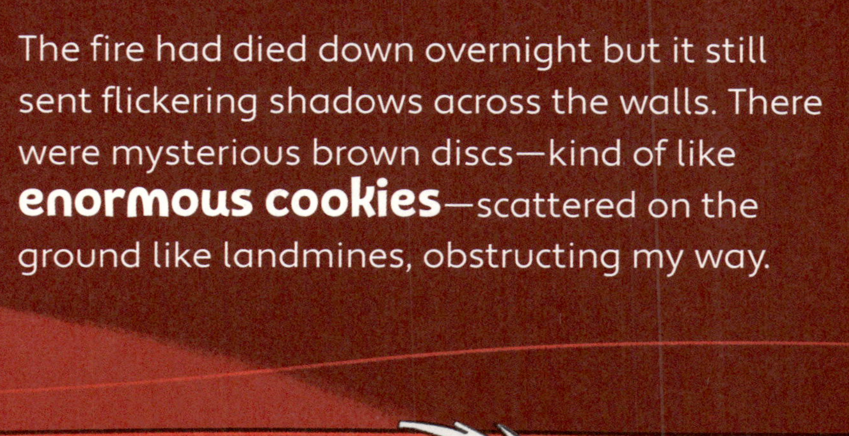

I pressed down gently on one. It was hard on the outside, with a thick gooey centre. I don't know why I thought a taste-test would be a good idea.

I **regret** it. Very much.

What I can now confirm, however, is that T-Bone is not toilet trained.

T-Bone didn't stir. I was worried he was asleep. I repeated myself but much louder. Still nothing.

Taking care to avoid the fake cookies, I crept around T-Bone's enormous frame to see his face better. He was watching me, but with disinterest.

'Aren't you going to **chase** me?' I asked. T-Bone merely closed his eyes.

The disguise wasn't working. My only option was to think of a plan B.
Hmmmmmmm.

I glanced around the barn for inspiration and spotted **Plus-Sized Puss**. She was sitting on a haystack beside T-Bone, purring loudly.
Purr-fect!

I kicked the stack so that the top crumbled, dropping Plus-Sized Puss right onto T-Bone's back. She immediately activated her best defence mechanism—her **claws!**

They dug into T-Bone's back and his eyes shot wide open.

He bellowed. The sound made Plus-Sized Puss dig in **deeper**.

T-Bone was on his feet in an instant. He ran for the door and I fled before him.

CHAPTER SIX

THE BLIND CHASE

I raced out of the barn with T-Bone in close pursuit. Plus-Sized Puss held on for dear life. I'd learnt a trick from Ringo. Rather than run directly to T-Bone's pen, I was going to **weave** left and right and follow a path with regular cover.

Tank to bull pen
Tree to shed
Shed to tank

'You can do it,' Billy **cheered**. 'I believe in you!' Billy's voice was enough to distract T-Bone. I watched in horror as the bull changed course. Instead of chasing me, he headed directly for Billy.

Run, Billy. He's coming right for you!

Who's coming right for me?

T-BONE!!!!

WHAT??!!
But I'm the cheerleader!

He doesn't care, run!

Billy didn't need any further encouragement. What he did need, though, was the ability to see past his floppy fringe.

He **crashed** into a fence.

He **crashed** into a wall.

He **crashed** into a tree.

He started **crying** and **screaming** and **hyperventilating** all at once.

T-Bone came for him, horns lowered.

'Turn right and run,' I called out.

Billy turned right and ran out into the open just in time. Unfortunately, he ran under the clothes-line and his horns picked up a **red shirt**.

Once again, T-Bone was off, now chasing the moving **red flag** that Billy had become. Billy veered to the left. He accelerated downhill and away from the bull pen.

'No, no, no,' I cried, chasing after them both. It was too late to turn Billy around.

At the bottom of the hill is a dam. A pump sends water up the hill for us to drink. We never drink directly from the dam because **leeches** live in it. In case you don't know what a leech is, it's basically a **vampire slug** and slugs were already gross to begin with. Once attached, leeches are very difficult to remove.

Billy ran into the dam and sank. T-Bone pulled up short and Plus-Sized Puss was thrown clear. She landed on Billy's head just as it reappeared above the water's surface. The claws went in again and Billy and Plus-Sized Puss **flailed** around in the water like a pair of terrible synchronised swimmers.

I bypassed T-Bone, who stood breathing heavily by the water's edge, and rushed around to the other side.

Billy managed to stumble out of the water and Plus-Sized Puss jumped free. The **enormous** cat hissed at me before high-tailing it back up towards the barn.

Billy's mohair, which we had spent so long brushing, now clung tightly to his heaving frame. I used my teeth to pull the **red** shirt from Billy's face.

He shook his head and his fringe swept to the side, revealing the fire of fury in his eyes. To make things worse, two **leeches** had attached themselves to Billy's face, positioned like **angry eyebrows**.

'I'm going to get you for this, Barny!' he screamed.

I didn't think I should let Billy know about the leeches. Not yet. Instead, I looked down at the wet **red** shirt still in my mouth and I had another **brilliant** idea.

CHAPTER SEVEN

RED FLAG

I turned to T-Bone, the **red shirt** hanging from my mouth. I waved it and saw T-Bone's eyes twitch. I waved it **furiously** and T-Bone scratched at the dirt with his front hooves. 'Stop doing that, you idiot, he's going to charge,' Billy said.

And charge he did.

I ran like I'd never run before. T-Bone was **faster** than me, but I was **craftier**. I twisted left and I twisted right.

I was smaller and could turn more easily. I moved in circles and at one point I even ran between T-Bone's legs.

The whole time, I waved the **red shirt** and it drove T-Bone mad with **rage**.

'**Woof**, **woof**, I'm a bad dog, come and get me,' I said through gritted teeth.

I made my way slowly but surely to T-Bone's pen. I was desperately trying to locate Shaama to make sure she was in place and ready.

I should have kept my eyes on T-Bone.

He swooped in and I got caught up in his horns. I spat the **red shirt** out and it flew over T-Bone's eyes. He turned suddenly and because we were going so fast, he **toppled** to the ground. I flew forward, skidding through grass and dirt.

When I came to a halt, I took a quick look around.

We'd tumbled right into T-Bone's open pen!

We were right where we needed to be! I could see Billy **rushing** down the road.

I escaped the pen and used my head to close the gate, by which time Billy was by my side. T-Bone rose to his feet. His nostrils **flared**.

'Quick,' I said to Billy. It took three attempts to hook the gate latch onto his horn.

'You did it!' I yelled.

Shaama took this as the signal. She hit the switch and **electricity** surged through the wire.

Unfortunately, Billy had not yet disentangled himself. As he jolted up and down, his wet hair once again stuck out in sharp spikes.

I hadn't realised we were being stalked by three of the old chooks until they leapt out of the bushes, revealing themselves.

'Quick, girls, now's our chance,' Rhonda shrieked. They flew onto Billy's back and started jolting along with him.

I found a nearby stick and threw it at Billy, knocking him and the chooks clear.

T-Bone grunted but remained still. He could hear the **buzzing** and knew what that meant.

'We did it! We did it! We did it!' I sang out. Billy was shaking and **steam** was coming off him.

The chooks were **jittery** with both excitement and leftover electrical charge.

'Oh my, I feel decades younger,' Lyn crowed.

'I'm practically a newborn chick,' Alice said.

'Just wait until Ethel sees us,' Rhonda added.

Together they hobbled off up the road, looking very dishevelled and slightly **charred** around the edges.

Shaama joined Billy and me, a huge smile on her face. She stopped when she saw Billy. 'Ummm, why do you have **leeches** as eyebrows?' Shaama asked.

'What?!' Billy turned to me.
'Oh yeah, sorry, I was going to tell you about that . . .'

The scream that came of Billy's mouth was loud enough to be heard in space.

CHAPTER EIGHT

SWEET DREAMS

By the time the humans woke up, we were sitting in our rightful position, by the fire, in the barn.

Billy had two large **red marks** above his eyes from where we'd pulled the leeches off. They hadn't come off easily. He'd lost some of his precious hair and skin in the process and I discovered he can **bite** even harder than Ringo can.

'Enjoy it guys,' I said. '**The Nerd Herd** has earned the prime position by the fire.'

'When did you start using that name?' Shaama asked.

I shrugged. 'If you can't beat 'em, join 'em. What do you think, Billy?' Billy turned away from me.

'Aww, don't be like that,' I said. 'Look what I've got.' I showed Billy the dead rat's ribcage that I'd picked up from outside. 'It's the **antique ivory hairbrush** we used on you earlier. Ready for another go?'

‘That is a bone covered with bits of **dead animal**. Please tell me you didn’t comb that through my hair.’

‘Ummmmm . . .’

We heard a growl and looked up to see both **Ringo** and **Plus-Sized Puss** standing before us.

'Don't mention it,' I said, with a flick of my tail.

'You don't belong here,' Ringo said. '**Scram**.'

'Actually, I think you'll find that we are the most **ferocious** animals here on this farm. Don't believe me? Ask Mrs Fox. Ask T-Bone.' The tremor in my voice added a very nice vibrato effect, I thought.

Plus-Sized Puss lifted a leg and extended her claws. 'Is that so?' she purred.

So, we slept curled around our tree, outside.

There's nothing quite like sleeping under the stars, is there?

Shaama spat at me.

That night, I had such a pleasant dream. I was wearing a crown and everyone was calling me King Barny. Ringo kneeled before me.

It was a wonderful, wonderful dream.

I woke up not able to breathe. My mouth was covered by a **bushy tail**.

I was seized around the neck and picked up. I tried **screaming** but couldn't get a sound out. I could see Shaama and Billy sleeping, oblivious to what was happening.

I was carried down the hill before the tail was removed from my mouth. I bleated as loudly as I could, but it was too late. I was picked up again and carried off into the night at a rapid pace. In the moonlight, I could just make out the red fur of my captor.

Mrs Fox had come to get her revenge.
And here I was, **stuck in her mouth!**

TO BE CONTINUED . . .

How will Barny get out of this one?

Will **Barny** ever see Shaama and Billy again?

Will Mrs Fox be having **lamb** for dinner?

Will Shaama ever deal with her **hoarding** problem?

Find out in:
The Nerd Herd 3: Outfoxed